IF YOU ARE A MALE UNDER 40, DO <u>NOT</u> READ THIS BOOK

THE SAVVY MAN'S GUIDE TO FINDING TRUE LOVE

Thomas Dunker

THE SAVVY MAN'S GUIDE
TO FINDING
TRUE LOVE

Thomas Dunker

Stormy River Publishing

Stormy River Publishing

ISBN: 978-0-578-02913-9

Cover Art: © Aledeane / Dreamstime.com

1

If you are a single male at least forty years old and looking for True Love, this book might open your eyes; if it doesn't, well, you're just not thinking straight. As soon as you begin reading it, you have put yourself on a path to greater happiness, and its message will be so obvious you'll be amazed you didn't see it for yourself. But, hey... I didn't figure it out right away myself either.

Everybody moves at his own pace and learns when they're ready to learn. I hope you're ready to learn.

I like to recall a conversation I had with my twin sister when I was in my late twenties, struggling to be smooth, suave, successful, and look like I knew what I was doing. It went like this:

Me: I go through so much trial and error, and some of it is really painful, not to mention outright embarrassing. I wish Dad had explained a lot of this stuff to me when I was younger so that I didn't have to learn it myself the hard way.

My sister: He did. You just weren't willing to listen at the time.

Well, dear reader, NOW is the time to listen to someone who knows something!

2

Being single and dating a lot of different women over a period of many years can be a lot of fun. I know because, for the most part, I've been doing it my whole adult life, a period that spans about forty years. Well, guess what? Being in a great relationship with one woman may be a lot more fun than dating around! But wait, there's more!

3

Having fun on a date or two or three is an important ability, but having fun with someone date after date after date over a long period of time is infinitely more fun because you can talk about all the fun you had later with that person, and you'll both know what you're talking about—and that's a lot of fun too, on top of the fun you had together!

Never underestimate the value of shared memories!

You'll discover, if you haven't already, that memories become more important as you age. Being able to share memories that go back over the years is lots of fun and enriches the moment, which is another reason you better give some more thought to being with one person from here on.

You are not getting any younger—fact.

Life is short, especially when you're having fun. And surely you must know this: you can live longer in a stable relationship with a lifetime partner. The statistics prove this.

The purpose of this chapter is to remind you of the superiority of having one great long-term relationship over having endless short relationships. One great relationship should be your goal; don't lose sight of that as you read on because this book will help get you to your goal. After all, isn't that why you're reading this? You probably should re-read this chapter and think about it even more the second time around.

4

Life can be rich, and by that I don't mean "rich" in the sense of great wealth—though that's a possibility too. I mean rich in the sense of fulfilling, rewarding, and filled with happiness and joy, which is out there for you. If a life like that doesn't interest you, then stop right now and hand this book to the man next to you. He'll be grateful because surely two of the biggest idiots in the world couldn't be standing next to each other.

Life is inherently rich actually, but if it doesn't seem that way to you, then you're not exactly doing it right. Doing it right entails a lot of things and covers a lot of territory. There are many, many—even countless—ways you can enrich your life so that when it is all over you can say it turned out to be a good one.

The stuff you read from here on basically refers to only one of those many avenues to a rich life, but it may be the most important one of all in giving you a rich life. Yes, the answer is love and, specifically, love in the sense of a meaningful life shared with someone, yes, till death do you part. True love is what I am talking about. Everyone wants that. If they don't, they're fools. If you don't, again, I say hand this book to the man next to you.

5

Life can be rich, like I said in the previous chapter. And, I ask you, who would be most likely to know that? Better question: who would be most likely to understand what it means to have a rich life? A ten year-old? No. A sixteen year-old? No. A twenty year-old? No. A thirty year-old? Probably not, though thirty year-olds should have a pretty good idea. They've been through a lot, but not as much as a forty year-old, as you will read shortly. Let's go with that age: people in their forties actually know quite a bit about life. I guess it takes more than thirty years to get that knowledge, but most people you talk to will agree with me on that point.

It is often said about a man, frankly, if he isn't successful by the time he's forty, he's probably in the wrong career. The same can be said of a woman, of course, at least in this country. The point isn't whether or not this is a test to determine if someone is successful; rather, the point is that forty seems to be a critical milestone in one's life, and rightly so.

You apparently are not yet in a successful "career" relationship... well, guess what? YOU have been doing something wrong! Dating endlessly should not be a career; that's called job hopping.

Everyone knows that hopping around like that is not a good thing for long-term success.

6

Thus, by the time a person is forty, he or she ought to have a pretty good understanding of who they are, what they like and don't like, and how life works. The learning curve for that achievement doesn't go much higher beyond the forties.

At forty years old, a person should know things, about themselves, about others, and how things work, and even about how life works. You should move to the next chapter so that you can be fully convinced about the value of being at least forty years old and, therefore, the value of dating someone who is at least forty years old.

7

In the following chapters, I've listed fifteen reasons why being at least forty years old counts for something when it comes to knowing about life. You must know the following is generally true about people in their forties, but I'm spelling it out for you anyway. You will find yourself nodding on most, if not all, of the reasons.

Reason #1

They probably have experienced death firsthand, possibly a parent, certainly a friend, heaven forbid a child. Not only do they surely know the heights of joy that comes with family and friendships, but they know the depths of sorrow as well. A little seasoning in life can be painful, but it's a good thing. You do it to your food; surely you should seek it in your relationships.

Reason #2

They probably have had successes and failures. They probably have been fired or lost a job unexpectedly, which is also a devastating proposition. A lot of soul-searching is just one of the benefits of devastating propositions. People who do this get to know themselves a lot better, which makes it easier for you to get to know them.

Reason #3

They probably have moved from one city to another, probably out of state, and probably more than once, so they know about starting over, setting up a new life, and making new friends in a land of strangers.

Reason #4

They probably have been in a hospital or two, face to face with a disease or some kind of malady or an injury beyond the cure of a self-applied bandage. People who have gone through these experiences are more in touch with life. They've had to give it more thought than most people, and one outcome of it is that they truly realize the tenuousness and fragility of life. There's a good chance they are more willing to embrace life,

which is good if you are looking

for a meaningful embrace!

Reason #5

They have scars, lumps, bumps, and stuff going on that happens to a body with experience and live with all that, without getting in too much of a huff. They have come to grips with the fact that their identity is something more than simply a body.

By the way, this works both ways. This reality should make it more likely that they will accept you because when you're over forty, it's not likely that your body is the most desirable thing out there in the world of men.

Reason #6

They have had their heart broken, maybe more than once— probably more than once.

Reason #7

They have been a victim of a crime, either firsthand or victimized as a property owner, for example.

Reason #8

They have helped a lot of friends through difficult times in many ways, maybe financially, maybe even emotionally, maybe even physically, maybe even in ways their friends don't know about or even understand.

Reason #9

They know about the power of
dreams, and they know that
dreams don't always come true.

Reason #10

They have found themselves many times in difficult situations that they never dreamed of and got through them.

Reason #11

They know that more of their lives are behind them than ahead of them, making time even more valuable.

Reason #12

They have seen enough surprises of all magnitudes to know that there are more surprises ahead, of all magnitudes.

Reason #13

They have probably outlived a pet, one they hugely loved.

Reason #14

They know about sex, at least more than they knew when they were in their thirties.

Reason #15

They have a sense of what things cost in life: what it costs to run a household; what extras costs, like life insurance or health care; what speeding tickets and car accidents cost; and what entertainment costs, like eating out and traveling. And, they know what mistakes can cost, too, because by the time someone is forty, he or she has made a lot of them.

8

People who have been around for at least forty years know a lot more about life than people who have been around for less time. They've seen a zillion more TV shows and lived through a zillion more newsworthy events. This should be easy for you to grasp— no argument on this point, right?

Well, it doesn't hurt to call attention to the fact that most people talk about their lives in a context. They say things like:

Do you remember where you were when that happened?

That was the year that changed everyone's life, wasn't it?

I'll never forget the way we all thought in those days.

Their music was a big influence in my life. Yours too?

Can you believe we all dressed like that!

Let's hope that the listener can relate to the context when the speaker makes statements like the above; otherwise, the full meaning is lost. Communication is hampered, maybe even truncated—ended.

9

Context is everything. The exclamation "Fire!" has countless meanings, all of which could have an impact on your behavior, most of them an alarming impact, depending on the context. For example, you wouldn't know how to react to the expression "Fire!" unless you knew that...

- You were in a movie theatre.

- You were on a firing squad.

- You were in front of a firing squad.

- You were manning artillery on the battlefield.

- Someone was pointing to your hair.

- Someone was running out of a house.

- Someone was running out of your house!

Or, if the word is used literally or figuratively, as in:

- She's on fire... burning up.

- She's on fire... getting everything right.

Or, another example:

- The market's on fire
  (the stock market when it's going up)

\- **The market's on fire**

(the grocery store when it's

burning down)

When a conversation between
two people suddenly slips into a
context that is not shared by the
two people, the connection
between them is lost and,
sometimes, the connection is
difficult to get back. Sometimes
you can't get it back. Dead space
doesn't help in the search for True
Love.

In all of these possibilities, it would be critical to know the context. In relationships, it is critical to know the context too.

You are required to pause here and re-read the above sentence and actually think about it until you realize the total and absolute sensibility that is behind it.

10

Conversations with dates are the same way: context is everything, especially in dating because gender differences might add a bit of confusion to the exact interpretation of words. Gender differences make shared context even more important to successful communication.

By the way, shared context comes from shared life experiences. This means that the more experiences that are shared, the more shared context there is, and with fully shared context comes understanding. And guess what? Understanding can be the basis of love, notably True Love!

Don't forget that!

11

Stop saying to yourself that "opposites attract" in seeking a long-term partner. That phrase has no foundation in meaningful relationships, though we use that nonsensical thinking all the time. Relationships are built on common ground, the basis of which is similar viewpoints, experiences, and strategies for handling life.

Of course, no one agrees on everything. Differences in opinion can add a little spice to a relationship, but don't kid yourself into thinking that opposites attract. IF you think they do, you are engaging in short-term behavior that means one unsuccessful relationship after another. You will become a hamster on the wheel, going nowhere fast. As I said, do not kid yourself because long-term relationships require that two people have a lot in common.

Don't be a hamster!

By the way, a forty year-old man and a twenty-two year-old women generally do not have a lot in common when looking at the big picture of life experiences. The mutual agreement on some issues, such as sex (e.g. "We both love sex.") and where you want to have dinner that night (e.g. "We both love Mexican.") accounts for only a couple of pixels in the billions of pixels that make up the big picture. A couple with that much age difference does not have much to say that could be described as a fully shared context.

If you are interested in True Love for a lifetime, don't forget the importance of context.

12

Let's talk a bit more about age, specifically your age. Age becomes less important the older one gets. Within this construct is the idea that age is important. A few comments are in order.

There is the man's rule of thumb about the age of the youngest woman he can go out with. The rule: a man should never date a woman younger than half his age plus seven. This is a formula that is well known among men and actually used by a lot of men as a guideline. It is also a formula that justifies a lot of foolish behavior.

You can talk about it with your friends, but don't ever believe it.

13

Since, dear reader, it is assumed that you are at least forty because you paid attention to the book cover's plea that men under forty years old should not be reading this, let's take the simple application of that rule-of-thumb formula to a forty year old man. It indicates that the youngest woman a man of forty could go out with is twenty-seven years old.

Any age younger than twenty-seven years old, slips the man below the formulaic age group and gets awfully close to the age of his children or, if he doesn't have any, his friends' children. That's not right and you know it. Not that that has ever stopped a man.

You have probably gone out with women younger than the formulaic boundary and why not? It's only a guideline. After all, it seems that men can go out with women much, much younger than themselves.

They can and they do. Let's talk about that.

(Let's **not** talk about the fact that your 40+ body cannot possibly be as enticing to much younger women as the bodies of men in their 20's and, probably, 30's as well. If you think so, you're delusional and, worse, totally focused on something that isn't all that important when it comes to True Love. You need to be beyond the idea that anyone's body is the basis for a relationship.)

First, significant age differences lack common ground in life context. That's a reason right there not to go out with someone much younger. Read Chapter Ten again.

Second, if you're at least forty and she's under forty, she probably knows less about life than you do, which is another reason not to go out with someone much younger. Read Chapter Seven again.

Of course, what I really want to say is that if your date is a lot younger than you, YOU probably know LESS about life than she does! Consequently, you need to pay careful attention to the guidelines presented in the next chapters. They will save you from the hamster wheel, keep you in touch with reality, and get you farther along the path to True Love.

14

Here are my age guidelines for dating, the ones I think you should pay attention to most, as a man who is at least forty years old:

Guideline #1

Never again go out with a woman under forty.

Guideline #2

Try to date within the age range of your age plus or minus three years (heeding the first guideline, of course).

Guideline #3

Re-read guidelines #1 and #2. They are the only guidelines you need to know regarding age when seeking True Love!

Think about those guidelines on age. They make sense. Given the importance of context, dating outside the plus/minus three-year range puts you into what I call another generation. In this case, I am suggesting that generations are not twenty-five year spans but really only seven year spans.

The three year difference in age in either direction from your age creates a full range of seven years, which was the range of kids you knew in high school from start to finish and in college as well, if you went to college. This range is an excellent measure of the context in which you grew up. Of course, as I said earlier, age becomes less important, but in the name of our search for True Love, I'm willing to defend the plus or minus three-year guideline for any

man over forty. It's your generation!

15

Now you have an idea of your dating parameters for an acceptable age group, along with the measures that give you something you never paid attention to before, the two measures that give you a much better understanding for the basis of a True Love relationship... you haven't forgotten have you? Comparable levels of experience *and* context! With this foundation, you are now ready to move into true enlightenment for finding your True Love.

16

First, the woman you should be seeking for True Love has already been married. That's right. This thought is so important that it must stand alone, so it gets its own paragraph. Read it below:

The woman you should be seeking for True Love has already been married!

Never underestimate the value of experience, especially marital experience. Of course, telling you that now might be a real eye-opener because up until now, in the world of dating, you probably haven't particularly cherished experience because, for whatever reason, you were most likely chasing women who hadn't had much experience in relationships. This is something like the blind leading the blind and together hoping they won't bump into anything.

Or, you went out with women who have had experience in relationships but didn't connect with you because you didn't get it: they were fearful of a relationship with you because it didn't appear that you cherished experience or even knew what a real relationship was all about.

But you are learning!

17

    Let's talk more about the goal of finding True Love by seeking a relationship with a woman who has already been married. And maybe you've been married too, but we're not going to talk about why you are no longer married. Your date will have to come to grips with that and decide whether or not it works for her. This is about finding True Love for you, so let's keep working in that direction.

As for going out with women who have been married, well, that's a good start. That's actually right thinking, as long as the reasons the woman is no longer married are good reasons.

Let's briefly identify some good and bad reasons for a marriage in the past, just to make sure you get the picture:

Good reasons she is no longer married:

- **Untimely death of a husband**

- **Abandonment by the husband**

- **Caught the husband cheating**

- **Child or spousal abuse by the husband**

- **Husband was into substance abuse**

Get the picture?

Bad reasons that she is no longer married:

- Got bored with her husband

- Husband didn't make enough money

- Other men were more exciting

- Wanted a new life without discussing it

- Couldn't buy everything she desired

- Caught cheating by the husband

\- **Husband didn't share drug habit**

Again, get the picture?

The examples of good and bad reasons for getting out of a marriage should help you realize that you need to be discerning in selecting a lifetime mate who has already been married. Maybe you knew that.

You have to be careful, as plenty of studies say that the likelihood

of success in a second marriage goes down. Statistics are always suspect and, besides, don't forget those numbers include people who didn't have the right goals in mind for seeking True Love, unlike you, once you've finished this book.

18

I certainly don't want to insult your experience with women and your general knowledge, but I am risking that because you are reading this book. This means you are wanting True Love and haven't been able to find it.

After reading this book, you can begin seeking it, and that's a good start, as long as you're looking in the right place. Already, after reading the first seventeen chapters, you may have discovered that you've been looking for love in all the wrong places. Now, you should have a much better idea what the right place is.

I'll say anything I can, fearless of offending you, if I believe it will help you reach the goal of True

Love. Most importantly, at this point in the book, you know that your True Love will have been married and that your attention now completely moves away from women *under* forty years old.

Forever.

Forever.

Forever.

Forever.

Hard to swallow the "forever" part? It shouldn't be IF you are thinking correctly. So, think about what you have read so far because it will make it easier for you to swallow. Repeat after me: I will never again go out with a woman under forty because I am interested in True Love.

Is a single woman *at least* forty years old who has never been married a potential partner for you? And what about the woman who is at least forty who has been married? The answer on both counts is absolutely yes! Do not discount those possibilities—especially since they include every available woman over forty!

19

But, as you will learn in the next chapter and beyond, the single-never-been-married women over forty are going to have some very tough competition for your affections and a lifelong commitment, for many very good reasons. And some of the women who have been married will have a battle of it too! Read on.

20

The next parameter for identifying your True Love is child's play. That's right. The True Love you should be seeking should be a mother with at least one child, of any age. This qualification is most commonly known as motherhood. That's right, you're best bet of finding True Love is by dating single mothers.

Mothers are superior partners. Yes!

Mothers are superior partners in comparison to single women and women who were formerly married but without children for lots of reasons. I've listed ten good reasons, one in each of the next ten chapters.

21

Reason #1

Mothers are superior because they are calm in the midst of chaos.

Children are prone to accidents. One might even argue that children are accidents waiting to happen. And things happen all the time. Even one child can mean a parade of visits to a hospital, endless calls to sitters, and layering of sudden needs on top of the usual household demands—all things that can lead to chaos. The only way the child can survive, along with everyone else, is for Mom to have a cool head when everyone else has lost theirs. Imagine the challenges of confronting chaos when more than one child is in the picture! Moms do that all the time.

Many, many times a cool head is required as a typical response to everyday activity. The little one is crying often enough even when danger is not imminent. When things get dicey, and everything that could possibly go wrong goes wrong, it's Mom who comes to the rescue. Moms know about chaos because they manage it practically every day. No household can survive without at least one cool head in the midst of chaos, and Mom has the cool head you can count on.

22

Reason #2

Mothers are superior because they know about nurturing.

Every man loves to be nurtured, but many men haven't really experienced what that means, at least not since they were very little. There is no contest in this world when it comes to identifying the person who is best at nurturing others. Moms are the nurturers, and their nurturing skills are in play at all times for everyone in the family because they can't help it: that's what moms do.

Moms innately know about caring for others. It's built into them, as it's built into all women, but its most powerful trigger for taking it to its ultimate expression is the birth of a child. From that point on, it just doesn't stop. Moms will tell you that nurturing is something that defines a mother; it becomes second nature. Fortunately, for the husband, the nurturing doesn't have limits in expression. Moms know the power of feeding, caring for, and working for the security of their loved ones, but they also know the power of a loving hug, a soft voice that soothes, and the touch of tenderness, all of which go into all aspects of caring for someone else—including you!

23

Reason #3

Mothers are superior because they put others first, including you if you are lucky enough to be in a relationship with one.

It's the way women are wired, and giving birth triggers the juxtaposition of who is more important, you or me? The birth of a baby immediately elevates the baby into the number one position for attention and, importantly, personal sacrifice and sublimation of personal needs for the satisfaction of another's needs. Moms know better than anyone else about putting others first, above themselves. This means that they get the concept of paying attention to others above themselves. In the long run, you'll benefit greatly from this concept.

Watch them carefully, and you will see that moms put others first. Oh? You're not sure what that means? Besides the typical guess that moms will pay attention to your needs (it's what moms do), putting others first means that they pay attention to everyone else's needs first. Maybe this is a glittering generality, but if you watch closely, you will see plenty of instances when your mom-date accords other people, including older people, children, and every other kind of person, a higher level of respect than you usually see from single, childless women, especially ones under forty.

If, as a single guy, you have never gone out with a single mom over forty, go try it immediately and pay attention. I say pay attention because within minutes, you will sense a different quality of interaction between the two of you than what you have experienced with single women under forty who do not have children. Yes, that's right, if you pay attention, you will feel the difference in no time.

24

Reason #4

Mothers are superior because they know the world is not all about them, unlike many, many women who have not been mothers.

It is easy enough to argue that in the dating world, in this country anyway, the single woman in the dating world believes it's all about her: her needs, her care, her safety, her happiness, and her sex life. Just listen to the TV show "Sex and the City," and you will get a perfectly clear idea of what I'm talking about.

With moms, it's a whole different story from your stories about dating women who are not mothers. When it comes to being in a relationship with a man and knowing what's important to a man, moms get it.

25

Reason #5

Mothers are superior because pain doesn't make them panic.

Moms know about pain, physical pain. No one likes it, of course. You know where I'm going with this point, don't you? You have never given birth to a baby. I'm not a doctor—I don't even play one on TV—but I've talked to enough women to know a little bit about the pain. Here's what I have learned. The pain of birth is so painful that right after giving birth to a baby, it is tempting for the mom to say never again do I want to experience such pain. But—and this is where it's a little tricky— the pain is so painful that the mind actually blocks out the memory of exactly how painful it was so that Mom can experience the joy of having another baby, if that's what she wants.

Or, put it this way: one woman attempted to describe to a man the level of pain a woman experiences when birthing a baby with these words:

It would be the same feeling for you if you sh#t a wheelbarrow full of bricks.

A wheelbarrow full of bricks? Now that's a level of pain I don't even want to think about. But here's what you can think about: mothers know about things we'll never know about, and they put themselves through things we don't want to. That takes an enormous amount of inner strength and focus. Those are admirable qualities in a relationship!

26

Reason #6

Mothers are superior because they are great organizers.

Mothers have to be great organizers. The lives of others are in their hands. As a consequence, they know the value of structure and organization. They have to know where their things are and everyone else's. This happens to be true because they do most of the set up work for the kids and for everyone else in the house. This concept is most simply put by remembering when you were a kid in the house you grew up in who you asked first for help in finding something you couldn't find. It was Mom.

I'll bet you rarely, maybe even never, started a sentence with these words: "Hey Dad, do you know where my..."

With their truly exceptional organizational skills, moms make a household happen, and by extension, a mom can make your life happen too.

27

Reason #7

Mothers are superior because they know the value of time management.

It is a well known adage that when you want to get something done, ask a busy person to do it. Mom is that person. Beyond her organizational skills, moms quickly become the true machinery behind the output of a household because they are a home's efficiency expert. Anyone with kids knows the value of the clock and how quickly times passes as the school bus is about to arrive, as doctor's appointments have to be scheduled, as afterschool activities need coordination, as babysitter's are due to arrive.

Moms are the great managers of time because they are the only ones paying attention to everyone's schedule, besides managing their own. Dates with single, childless women, especially those under forty, mean a lot of waiting for the guy. Waiting, waiting, and more waiting. With moms over forty with kids, a man is dealing with a woman who has run a life with a schedule that waits for no one. Be with a woman who knows how to make it happen.

28

Reason #8

Mothers are superior because nothing grosses them out.

I don't know if it's the birth thing or the baby thing or some other thing, but moms don't get grossed out like women who haven't had kids. Everybody knows that. You do too, but you don't think about it.

Moms don't think twice about changing a diaper, cleaning vomit off a dinner plate, wiping a diarrhea-suffering child's butt, or dealing with the grossest mess you can think of. Moms just do it. They don't particularly like doing it, but liking or not liking it has nothing to do with Mom's behavior when there is something that a mom has to do. It's what moms do.

Generally speaking, dealing with gross things is not what women without children volunteer to do. And if women without children deal with gross things, it's not likely that they're doing it without flinching! In the world of gross, moms don't flinch. That's just one more thing about what makes moms special. They have seen it all and handled it. Now that is something to respect!

29

Reason #9

Mothers are superior because they pay attention to what everyone likes, especially YOU. And they remember it.

It comes with their management skills. Moms pay attention to details and remember what they have to remember, knowing that it will come up again. You see, moms have a different orientation than women without children: they operate on the assumption that they will see their child year after year, so they log key information into their memory banks. In effect, they train themselves to remember information that comes into play again and again, such as birthdays, anniversaries, foods that are liked, foods that are not liked, favorite activities, and favorite things of any nature.

Moms remember things for their children who will be forever part of their lives. This training to remember things makes it easier for them to include key information about you too that can be easily stored in their memory. It's what moms do. It's not as easy for women who do not have children to remember your needs, likes, and dislikes—they haven't had the training for that memory game.

30

Reason #10

Mothers are superior because they do motherly things that remind us of our mothers, who loved us more than anyone in the whole world.

Mothers can't help being motherly, even with their True Love. A woman's identity as a mom is so much a part of her identity as your True Love that it will undoubtedly include a little bit of an angle on mothering, and that's a good thing. That never hurt anybody, and you'll know exactly what I mean the first time you are laid up in bed with a bad cold or the flu.

31

You should have learned a lot by now. Your path for finding a partner you can call your one True Love has been laid out in front of you. It is an obvious path, too, one that is so obvious that it is hard to believe that it has been overlooked by you and so many men over forty years old over the years.

Perhaps you should chalk up your blindness to the obvious path to True Love to the way you are wired. Through the vast majority of millennia of our evolution, we men didn't really have an expectation of living much beyond thirty. Our success as a species depended on males, over millions of years of evolution and long ago, outperforming other males in a manner that allowed the strongest, fittest, smartest, etc. to win the prize: as much sex as you wanted with any women you wanted to have sex with, which, I suppose is still wired into our brains as the ultimate fantasy. That kind of fantasy is so deeply encoded into our DNA that it will still be there in another million years. At least.

Get a grip, man! The days of living in caves or hovels or stone buildings without heating are over (let us hope). The days of life expectations of only thirty years are over too (let us hope).

You have evolved. For a change, as a man over thirty-nine years old and living with the expectation to be around for many more years, you have a chance to really think about what makes you happy. The operative words in that sentence are *really think* because if you do really think about it and think about your desire for True Love (the most satisfying, most wonderful, most fulfilling thing in the history of mankind), then you will know where True Love lies from here on.

Don't

let

the

cave

man

in

you

rule.

Let

your

common

sense

rule!

Your salvation is with single moms who are at least forty years old.

But wait, there's more!

32

You thought I was done lecturing you, didn't you? Well, I'm not, and I don't think any of what I've written is a lecture. It's just common sense, and I'm sharing it with you.

All kinds of studies support the following, and it's just the tip of the benefits iceberg:

Married people have more sex and a better quality sexual relationship, in case you were wondering—that was probably the first thing on your mind, wasn't it?

33

I've intentionally kept this book and its message simple for a reason: the message is simple and it makes perfect sense. And you know it. So, go find that woman who is going to be your True Love and, when the time is right, marry her. And you will find her because you finally know what to look for:

A single mom at least forty years old who is single for the right reasons and happens to be within three years of your age, but NOT under forty. Now get with the program and go find her!

THE END OF THIS MESSAGE...

BUT, IF YOU ARE A SAVVY MAN, THEN THIS IS A NEW BEGINNING FOR YOU!

Appendix

THREE SHORT STORIES FROM

Confessions of a Dating Fool

by Thomas Dunker

Following are three short stories (chapters) from my book *Confessions of a Dating Fool*, about three dates: Carol, Julie, and Jill. I think they stand on their own as fun reading, but since you are now the enlightened seeker of True Love, read each one and ask yourself, What happened? Ask yourself why none of these women qualified as eligible women for True Love for me. Of course, as of this writing, I now know better!

CHAPTER 3: An Online Date in Scottsdale

Her name was Carol.

I am an attractive, affectionate, fit and athletic, fun-loving woman who is looking for someone special. I am currently separated, with my divorce finalizing soon. I'm basically a sunny, happy, successful person who looks at life with an optimistic viewpoint. In general, I am a calm and balanced person, but when I have fun, I go all out!

That's how she described herself in her online dating profile. She said a lot more about herself, of course, but the above was her opening gambit, the part that caught my attention. Fit and athletic are particularly important to me because I'm fit and athletic. I like fun-loving too. Success is good, and so is balance. Might be something here!

In online dating, someone's description and picture are very important. It's all you have to go on for that decision to proceed or not. And yet, in my experience, almost everyone lies to get that first meeting. Then what? Sometimes it works and sometimes it doesn't; but when it doesn't, expectations are unfilled and that, my friend, is the definition of anger, which is not a good emotion to create when meeting someone!

Carol's photo got me interested enough to open the profile and find out more about her. There was only one photo, which is tricky because one photo can leave a lot of room for misrepresentation, intentional or not. I like to see several, especially ones that show full body shots, preferably in a context of activity, along with the usual close-up of the face. More photos mean more honesty and more information, making the decision to contact or not a lot easier.

Carol had only one photo. Ordinarily, that would be a red flag, but that one photo was tantalizing, even if she was a little too obscure for me to really see what she looked like or get a sense of her. She wasn't doing anything in the photo, just sitting at the end of a table with her elbow propping up her chin, trying to look sexy no doubt, but achieving only wistfulness and borderline boredom, at least that's what I read into it. Ordinarily, that would be a red flag, but like I said, the photo was tantalizing. She had nice hair, flowing and shaped, with some wave that was a bit out there, almost breezy, but not too out there. It was nice. She had a look about her that I liked, a look that's hard to describe, like someone who knew about the sweetness of a nice life but was seasoned by independence and rich experiences. Wow, isn't it amazing what we think we see in a photo! I guess that's why they say a picture is worth a thousand words.

Another thing I liked about her photo was that she looked reasonably stylish, if stylish could be inferred from a black v-neck sweater, which was the only clothing item I could see. Ordinarily, limited input like that would be a red flag, but that one photo was—yep—tantalizing, even if black killed all the shadows that could reveal something about her figure.

I reread her profile again, a little more carefully this time, trying to ferret out some extra insights. There was a lot to like about it, although the fact that she wasn't actually divorced yet was a bit of a concern. Ordinarily, that would have been a red flag too, but the photo grabbed me, even though she might still be emotionally unsettled from the break up of her marriage.

There were a lot of possible red flags, but like I said, the photo was tantalizing. It was a tough call, but I decided to pursue contact, so I sent her an invitation online to meet me in person over an adult beverage. I didn't want to spend time exchanging endless emails and phone calls before meeting her. I'd done enough online dating to know that the frequency and amount of contact before meeting someone had little to do with an ultimate attraction. If there isn't chemistry in the first five seconds of meeting, whatever went on in all that foreplay of emails and phone calls won't matter.

Yep, chemistry is king, and both parties have to feel it at first sight or the goal shifts to ending the meeting as quickly as possible. Of course, having chemistry doesn't necessarily mean that two people are meant for each other; it just provides the necessary green light to proceed in exploring the potential. Granted, sometimes, though rarely, a relationship can blossom without chemistry up front, but it doesn't work that way with me ever—unless you count Celeste, that goofy plain Jane of a girl in my high school who, three years later, turned out to be the hottest cheerleader at the University of Wisconsin. But that's an ugly duckling story, and they're endemic to our childhoods.

Carol's simple single photo worked for me. Did I say it was tantalizing? Oh, a million times already. Anyway, she agreed to meet me. We set a time and day: Thursday at six o'clock at Houston's restaurant, at the bar. It was the Houston's in Scottsdale on Scottsdale Road, a very popular watering hole for Scottsdale's chic over-thirty crowd. The lights were always low, the kind of low that made you pause six feet inside the door so that your eyes could adjust. It was so dark that visibility didn't improve much even after they adjusted. This meant that everyone started looking better the instant they walked in.

I got to Houston's ten minutes early, which is typical timing for me on dates. Of course, the suspense was building, like it always does when meeting someone for the first time, someone you want to like, especially when meeting someone who gave you only one photo to work with, tantalizing as it was. That's the operative word in this story: tantalizing. I love that word. According to the dictionary, it means to excite by exposing something desirable while keeping it out of reach.

Anyway, six o'clock came and went, and she was now ten minutes late, still out of reach. In another five minutes she would no longer be fashionably late but chalked up as a no show. That's never a good start for a relationship, but it happens. It didn't happen this time, however, as a lone woman walked in and paused about six feet inside the door. My radar instantly identified her as the Carol I knew from the flip of her hair in the photo.

My radar is great for identification, but it also works for assessment, and my first impression was not a good one: Tantalizing didn't come through the door with Carol. There was nothing tantalizing about her figure, even in the low lighting. She was a lot closer to fat than fit. This wasn't a good start.

She walked right up to me, being easily identifiable at six foot three inches tall and bald, and smiled with a queried look, head slightly tilted down and eyebrows up, as if to say, "Is that you?" I put the greeting out first.

"Carol," I said with total confidence, "how nice to meet you. I'm Tom." And in a microsecond, I thought, "Now I'd like to go home," but the minimum commitment was for a drink that I'd pay for, like most guys do on a first-time online date. Who knows—maybe her personality would shine, and its light would blind my superficial reaction to her? I decided to give her the benefit of a doubt.

"Hi," she said. "Nice to meet you too."

She had a mushy three finger handshake, something that men generally don't like because they're so into firm handshakes as a factor in character assessment. And, she said nothing about being late. Ten minutes late was borderline okay, but an apology would have set her up as Miss Polite and respectful of my time, which would have been two good points on the scorecard. First impressions aside, my polite nature was determined to seek the good in her to make this meeting worthwhile, however unlikely it was that there'd be a second one. I was committed to a pleasant exchange, which is a good thing in a world that's often short on civility.

We seated ourselves at the bar for what could be called the obligatory drinks. After placing an order for a couple of glasses of an inexpensive Chardonnay that was agreeable to both of us, we jumped into a conversation that went in and out with snippets something like this:

"So," I opened, "isn't this online dating a trip? What an adventure it is."

"Yeah," she smiled in apparent agreement. I was looking for more from her, but not getting it didn't disappoint me. Our meeting was looking like a dead end, so I'd take what I could get and not worry about working the conversation.

"Have you had much luck in meeting guys you like?" I asked.

"No, not really," she sighed, making me wonder if I was included in that judgment. "Have you met anyone you liked?"

"Actually, I did," I said. "Last year. We dated for almost a year and broke up a month ago." Carol didn't interrupt, expecting more apparently. I decided to give her a little more: "She had a lot of nice qualities, but it wasn't meant to be." Now Carol perked up on that. I figure girls always want to know what went wrong with your last relationship so that they can discover if it's something that won't work for them. I had her attention.

"Why'd you break up?" she asked, clearly curious.

"We had a lot of fun together, but we also had some big differences."

"Like what?" Her curiosity was growing. It was a question that left me with a lot of latitude in answering. I could make a general statement, like we had different goals in life or not enough in common. Or I could throw out a racy fib, like she decided she was a lesbian, but I opted for something closer to the truth: "She was very religious, and I'm not," I stated in a matter-of-fact tone, but that didn't even get a lift of her eyebrow.

"Oh," she said, "does that mean the sex was bad?"

I thought that was a curious comeback and wondered what the segue was. Online dating left the door open for all kinds of questions that would never be asked in the normal decorum of a date.

"No," I said, and made that a one word answer to her question and quickly moved to new territory—her territory. "You said in your profile that you were looking to start a new business. Like what?"

"Matchmaking."

"Really?"

"Yeah. I'm good at fixing my friends up."

"Any of them get married?" I asked.

"No."

"Then how do you know you're good at it? Isn't matchmaking about marriage?"

"Not necessarily. It could just be about having fun. Maybe it leads to marriage. Maybe it doesn't."

"Okay. Maybe. Maybe you could make a business of it," I said, agreeably.

"Well, I don't know," she said, clearly unsure of herself. "I mean, maybe I could help people find their soul mate."

"Yeah, but you think you can do it for a living?" I hate the word soul mate, which may have tainted my tone. It's such a chick word, but I get it. I'd just never use the word myself.

"What—you don't think I can?" She must have read a little skepticism into my comment.

Our meeting could have turned south here because, of course, I didn't think she could be a matchmaker—she couldn't even "match" herself—but I was determined to keep it nice. "Look, I don't know you and, you know..." I scratched my eyebrow and looked around the room, hoping for some enlightenment or relief. I continued, a little more upbeat, "Well, who knows, maybe you'd be great at it." This was the best I could do while continuing to sound interested.

Getting through a drink was quickly becoming a big challenge. I wasn't sure I could do it. We hadn't had any awkward silences in our conversation up to this point, but they would be making an appearance soon, I was sure. There was absolutely no chemistry, and I was sure she sensed it too.

We had only been together ten minutes when I noticed her wine glass was empty. I decided to let it stay that way, from the point of view of my wallet. My glass is half full, but I'm feeling it should be empty, that I should down it, grab the check, and dash for the door. But I trudged on with our vapid conversation. My growing disinterest must have been evident, so I smiled a lot. Smiling is a great mask. I read some study that pointed out how an insult could be delivered without repercussions as long as it was said with a smile. People, it concluded, were more prone to react to what they saw than to what they heard. My smiling helped both of us.

Short of insulting her, I actually thought about challenging her on the "fit and athletic" claim in her profile. I get a little testy with online dates when their profiles stray dramatically from the truth. I was a sip away from challenging her. I held off, but only for a few seconds.

"Carol, writing a profile for this online stuff can be challenging." I began that sentence not intending to actually confront her, but I was suddenly possessed by a devilish combination of curiosity and the pursuit of truth, and continued: "And," I paused, "in your profile, you claimed…" I looked inward and asked myself how I could put this nicely. I leaned back a bit to finish the sentence, maybe to physically distance myself from her, paused, and started over: "Well, you claimed you're fit and athletic, and I don't really see that," I said, swallowing tenuously, ready to get my head taken off. "Maybe I misread your profile?" There I put it out there, asking for her wrath, surely, or some riposte of an insult directed at me.

"No, you read that right. I am fit and athletic. I play tennis once a week." No offense was taken. It was her truth, apparently.

"Oh, yeah, great," I replied, nodding in agreement and smiling, as if a moment ago I was just confused. "Yeah, you must be fit and athletic…definitely…tennis is demanding." I backed off and immediately understood that she saw herself that way and that I'd been a cad to go there. Even so, I still didn't think her description was honest, but like I said, it was her truth. I saw a different truth. For some reason, I think fit and athletic skews closer to aerobic instructors, but that's me and my own weirdness.

"What else do you do, Carol? Got other plans for a business?" She didn't seem to mind that abrupt switch to another topic, particularly since I sounded so interested. I was smiling.

"I don't tell people this, at least not when I first meet them, but…you wanna hear?"

I knew she was going to tell me, no matter what I said, but I was still being civil, so I lied and said, "Yeah, of course, tell me."

"I can tell people's past lives just by looking at them." She paused for a reaction from me. Clearly, this was a hit or miss statement for her with guys, so she paused and looked at me, wondering how I'd take this news. I took it, determined not to openly flinch or roll my eyes, and I took another sip of wine to get me closer to the end of this date. I should have just gulped the rest down, tossed a twenty on the bar, and walked out right then.

"Really," I replied, "You can tell me about my past lives just by looking at me? Right here? Right now?" My civil tone was still operative because I didn't even remotely believe in past lives and declined to tell her what a bunch of nonsense all that was to me. I'm now convinced that we are so not for each other. I smiled some more, waiting for her next statement, willing to ride this one a little longer, but eyeing the bartender, hoping he'd see that I was ready to give him my credit card. He didn't.

Carol then reached over her empty wine glass to get to mine, picked it up, put it to her lips, and just before taking a sip, looked at me and said, "Do you mind?" seeking permission to have some of my wine. I didn't mind at all. It might get us to the end of the date sooner.

"No, go ahead. Enjoy," I said at the same time she drained my glass. I could have said, "There's always more where that came from," but I didn't. I wondered if she thought that would trigger a request to the bartender for another round. Wonder or not, I didn't see another round as a possibility. I don't recall a date ever grabbing for my wine and polishing it off, but there's a first time for everything, and online dating has surprised me and a lot of others with first times. Now, we both had an empty glass in front of us, which for me was the green light for my departure. I turned to her, contemplating the approach I should take for making our first meeting our last meeting.

She was looking directly into my eyes, as if she was trying to see the bottom of a well, something beyond my aqueous humor, making a thorough but assuredly fruitless penetration of my pupils, the windows into my psyche, perhaps.

"I can see only one past life in you," she said. "Usually I see more, but with you, I see only one."

"I'm new to this universe," I said smugly. I stopped talking while Carol kept looking deeply into my eyes. The suspense was killing me. I broke the silence between us: "What is it? What do you see?" I asked.

She peered into my eyes a few more seconds, no doubt truly striving to see into the very depths of my soul. I wondered if she could see anything at all, like my disinterest or the threshold for the end of this date. I admit, however, I was curious what past life she saw in me. I like baloney. It's funny stuff, though not very nourishing.

"What is it?" I repeated, as if my existence depended on knowing immediately. "What's the past life you see?"

She leaned back and slipped into a sobering tone, apparently not wanting to be taken lightly. "You're not going to like it."

"Try me," I said fatalistically, with the introduction of a nuanced tone of skepticism. "Just don't tell me I was Napoleon. Too many other people were Napoleon."

"I don't know if I should tell you."

I think she wanted me to beg at this point. I asked one more time, careful to sound like I was NOT begging. "What was my past life? You can tell me, and it won't hurt my feelings. I swear."

I waited through more of her ripening silence before imploring her yet again, my impatience surely leaked, "What? Was I Jack the Ripper?" I said sardonically.

"No," she said and paused again, looking fearful of telling me.

I refused to ask again and opted for waiting her out. Twenty seconds passed, which was all the time it would have taken to say, "I gotta go—bye!" Instead, I didn't move. I waited, patiently, with a dumb smile of feigned interest and anticipation on my face.

She leaned forward, looked to her right and then to her left and then into my eyes. "You were a Nazi," she declared.

"Really?" I said, feigning a gasp. "Now that's some kind of nasty past life, don't you think?"

"Yeah, that's why I was afraid to tell you."

"You really see that?"

"Yeah. It's in your aura."

On this news, I thought I should go to the Mayo Clinic for an aura check. Immediately. What a wacko! I wasn't going to dignify her vision with a plea for more. All I could say was, "Interesting. Napoleon would have been better." Her declaration was beyond my concept of civility. I thought to myself, "What a stupid thing to say upon meeting someone." It was time for me to go.

"Yeah," she quickly added, "but now, in this lifetime, you are a very nice person. I can see that. You are a really, really nice person."

"Well, thank you, Carol." That was better, but it wouldn't slow my exit. I responded sincerely and, again, with a smile, "I've enjoyed talking to you, but we probably should part ways."

"No!" she suddenly exclaimed loud enough to turn a few heads, as if the idea was totally foreign to her, as if the strength of her exclamation could negate my impending departure. It had the same soulful, reverberating ring to it as the "No" that I'd gotten from my last girlfriend when I told her our relationship had unraveled.

"Yeah," I repeated, "I think it's time to go." That was the truth, and I added, "It was nice meeting you, though," which wasn't the truth.

Then she looked at me again, as if searching for yet another past life in me, and then surprised the hell out of me by saying, "You want to come back to my place?"

Her question could have only meant one thing. Wow. Talk about not being on the same wavelength! Dating is such an adventure. We stared into each other's eyes. Mine were surely looking stunned, as if I'd just been Taser-ed, or maybe like a doe caught in the headlights on a Wisconsin highway at midnight. I imagined myself going with some deep-seated male instinct and saying, "Sure, let's go to your place!" Guys could be such dogs.

Instead, I said, "Thanks, really. I gotta go." I pulled a twenty out of my wallet, slapped it on the bar, rose up from my bar stool, dodged her with a two-step move, and walked out of Houston's with a squint from the bright light of the real world.

CHAPTER 8: A Sunset in Naples

Her name was Julie.

She lived in Charlotte, North Carolina, and I lived in Napa, California, just a little north of Charlotte and another twenty-seven hundred miles to the west. Dating, if that was in the stars, with this kind of distance between us was going to be a challenge, especially because I wasn't a big believer in long-distance dating. When I lived in New York, many years before that, anyone living more than ten blocks away was geographically undesirable because there were a million singles within ten blocks. But since neither of us lived in New York, maybe this would work.

I liked her right away. Most of all, I liked her eyes. They sparkled when I looked into them, past the blue. And she was smart—really smart—which made her really interesting. She had her own business, and it was a big one—a big furniture business, with lots of outlets in the Southeast. It didn't hurt that she was really cute—a pixie blonde who looked as good as anyone could look in a tennis dress. She was good at that too. Julie was good at everything.

Our first two dates were relatively short ones, both dinner dates. The first dinner was with ten other people at a private party on a late summer night in an Atlanta home with mutual friends. That wasn't an official date. However, because it was a subtle fix up, I'd say it could count as one. We were the only single people there, and it was the intention of our hosts for us to meet, and in a way, that's a date. That's where we met, and after we did some serious, but discreet, kissing later in the house, tucked behind a door in the seclusion of a distant den, it became a date, incontestably.

Kissing in our friends' den was fun. It was the culmination of having been very flirty with each other from the beginning of the evening, or as our host said, "from the gitgo." Sometimes it's easier to be flirty when the likelihood of seeing that person again is slim. It makes you less inhibited. We both knew we were geographically undesirable for each other, which in a funny way, translated into making the most of the moment. And yes, sometimes flirting with someone from elsewhere allows one to be a little more out there, a little more reckless, a little more liberal with words that go nicely with flirting. We were having fun spinning in the immediate sphere of a dozen people in the house, who were beginning to pick up on our chemistry. The fact that we were the only ones there who weren't married might have put a spotlight on us. Married people often live vicariously through singles, in my humble opinion.

Ducking away from the group without having our absence noticed wasn't possible, and as a twosome under each other's spell, our cover story of "taking a quick tour" of the house to get a few minutes by ourselves begged for speculation and all kinds of cat calls as we left the group. Of course, we maintained a sense of civility while in proximity to each other in front of our friends. However, once in the seclusion of a distant den, civility was overrun by a skyrocketing mutual attraction and that wonderfully intoxicating sensation of lust. We kissed slowly at first and then moved it up a notch, then another notch, and then another. We got swept away as much as two people standing in a friends' den at a fancy dinner party could, which is to say we kissed intensely. We couldn't help ourselves. We were lost to each other momentarily and frantically, swept away, kissing for about five breathtaking minutes before decorum demanded that we reengage with our hosts and the other guests. No one knew precisely what we'd been up to for the five minutes we'd been gone, but everyone had a pretty good idea! When we rejoined the group, Julie's face was crimson, and I looked like the cat that had just ate the canary.

An hour later, the party ended, and Julie drove away with the couple she had come with, discreetly blowing a kiss to me through the window as she faded from my sight. She and I expressed interest in seeing each other again, but neither of us knew when that would be, so we parted without specific plans. Minutes later, I thanked my guests for the fun evening and the fabulous introduction, and then drove back to my hotel in Buckhead, which is Atlanta's chic neighborhood and the home of too many great restaurants, clubs, and bars. I was energized and sorely tempted to party on, but the need to be fresh for an early business meeting the next morning forced me to my room, which was a shame because Buckhead is loaded with temptations, and they're almost all blonde.

Our second date, which was our first real date, happened four weeks later without a whole lot of planning. This time I was in Charlotte on short notice for business and was able stay over an extra night. One night there was a must for my meetings with clients. The other night was optional, and with Julie as an option, I booked it. I called her and was happy to learn that she could go out with me that second night. It was a Wednesday, and she was busy early in the evening, so we simply arranged to meet each other for a late dinner at The Palm at Phillips Place, where patrons jokingly say, "It's where the elite meet," but you know they're not really joking. The Palm has just the right amount of everything, which was why it's had this reputation for so many years. It was exceptional in every way.

Our dinner together was a lot of fun, and the evening went by way too quickly, which is the hallmark of a great date. I was cognizant that it was a school night and that Julie had three little children at home: a five, a seven, and an eight year-old, already sound asleep under the watchful eye of the sitter. Julie told me how sweet and adorable they were over dinner. Thankfully, she didn't talk too much about them. Most people say that talking too much about children when the other doesn't have them isn't advisable, especially on the first or second date, and I would have to agree with that. We got past the first date, and we would get through this one, but I wasn't sure about the future because sometimes kids are a deal-breaker in the long run, though not always, of course. It depends on what the kids are like and how mom integrates them into the relationship. All this was something to think about, but not that evening.

We flirted with each other through every course, talking about the things we would do on our next date— maybe a weekend adventure without her children (I wondered if she thought taking them along was an option.) We started naming our favorite places. Aspen? (No, it was too early in the season for snow.) Bermuda? (No, it was too far away for me.) San Francisco? (No, it was too far away for her.) Her home or mine? (No, it was too early in the relationship for home visits.) Naples in Florida, where her parents had a house? (Yes, for all kinds of reasons and no hotel bill!) We didn't decide on anything, but it didn't matter; we were having fun just thinking about having fun.

I paid the bill and walked her to her car with my arm lightly draped over her petite shoulders. At six foot three, I towered over her, so the arm-in-arm thing didn't work, but we didn't need that to feel the chemistry. It was still there; we just couldn't do anything about it that night. She had to go home because it was already late for a school night, which meant no ducking into someone's den tonight or making out in the car. That wasn't in the stars for either of us. We did kiss at her car door, however. And it was a really nice one, both of us imparting a moist, luscious long drawn-out message that we should see each other again. It's amazing what one can say with a kiss.

She got in her car and drove away. I got in my car and did the same, while wondering if I could do this long-distance thing and whether or not I could date the four of them: Julie and her three children, an all or none proposition, like it is with every mom. I didn't have to answer that question just then, but I knew I'd have to answer it at some point. Or maybe not. Maybe I could just let it fade away with the passage of time, making no answer the answer, and date someone else, making Julie just a memory.

Two months later, at home, Napa was damp and squishy from winter rain. The vines were bare and dark, almost black from being so wet. The vineyard floor was muddy. Too many gray days were starting to have an effect on me that wasn't pleasant. This was the Napa Valley that people don't see in postcards. It was still beautiful in its own way, just very gray—and very brown. And a little dull because it was the time of year that the vines just sit there and do nothing, and I felt I was doing the same. It had been six weeks since my trip to Charlotte and my dinner at The Palm with Julie. I hadn't been in touch with her at all: no emails, no phone calls, no nothing. Frankly, I had other things on my mind, like local girls and a lot of business, but not a lot of excitement.

Then one afternoon, a UPS truck pulled into my driveway and delivered a box big enough for some ice skates (a childhood point of reference from growing up in Wisconsin), but of course, it wasn't a box of ice skates. North Carolina was printed on the return address. It was from Julie. I opened it immediately and discovered a carefully wrapped bottle of champagne and two champagne flutes, accompanied by a handwritten note on girly, pink stationery, which said:

Let's party in Naples! Call me. xox, Julie

Timing is everything when it comes to relationships. I called her right away. We picked a weekend two weeks out. I hung up and then booked a flight to Naples, where she'd pick me up at the airport in the late afternoon to begin our long weekend at her parents' beach house. I was jazzed just thinking about a sunny weekend in a beach house. Being with Julie made it even nicer, of course.

Two weeks later, I landed in Naples. Julie met me outside of the baggage claim, in a black Mercedes sedan, one with a big number on the trunk lid. I guessed she liked to rent big. Or maybe it came with the beach house. Either way, like Julie, it was first class.

153

Twenty minutes later, we were driving up the gulf shore, and three miles later she turned into the entrance of a secluded driveway and pulled right up to a massive iron gate, which was opening with hydraulics that could lift a draw bridge. I think she paused longer than necessary so that I was sure to get the full effect. The gate must have been ten feet high with more scrolls than The Dead Sea. Then she zipped through it and came to a sudden stop, right at the front door, one hundred feet later. I thought this all might be a joke she was playing on me, pulling into some kind of museum. It looked a lot like The Frick Mansion in New York—I'm not kidding—but maybe bigger. She looked at me and hopped out of the car before I could say anything, ran around to my door, yanked it open, grabbed my arm, pulled me out to a standing position, and facing the mansion's front door with her arms straight out in front of her, palms up, announced, "Here we are." Then she sung out softly, "Ta-Daaaaa! My parents' place!" and laughingly exclaimed, "and they never use it!" as if they were fools. I instantly changed my mind about what constitutes a beach house.

Julie swiftly skipped up the front stairs with a key in one hand, unlocked the right side of the massive front door, and with a push, it swung open. I hopped up the stairs in pursuit, spellbound. My luggage could wait.

As the right side of the twelve-foot high Rococo door opened wide on its own momentum, I lost mine and stood mouth-open, slack-faced, and totally stunned on the threshold of the foyer of her parents' truly palatial home. I didn't say anything. I couldn't have if I wanted to; I was overwhelmed by the opulence before me. For the first twenty seconds, I just stared. Julie was surely enjoying my non-reaction and just let me be me. I was truly speechless, as I took in her parents' second home, or was it their third home, or maybe it was their FOURTH home? Whatever number it was, I now knew what Julie meant when she told me her father was a force. It had to be the biggest and possibly most beautiful home in Naples, Florida or anywhere in Florida. Palm Beach didn't have anything like this, though Trump's Mar-A-Lago, the old Merriweather Post mansion, was in the same league in size.

I could see past the foyer into a ballroom-sized living room done up in white on white on white across at least fifty feet of white marble, which floated an oasis of white carpet. My eyes moved beyond a continuous row of very tall sliding glass doors right out to an Olympic-size San Simeon-like pool surrounded by—by what? a dozen Greek statues? ancient philosophers? Athenian guards? Plato and his pals? And beyond their posturing was the Gulf of Mexico, forever sparkling, as if blanketed with a million floating diamonds.

Enough time passed for me to pull out of my state of suspended animation and finally say something, so I turned "Wow!" into five syllables, like a muffled coronet. I figured she had already heard anything else I could say a hundred times before from others. My drawn out "Wow!" said it all.

I took a deep breath, looked across the vast expanse of a fabulous decor, and mustered up a few more words, as I looked directly at her and calmly stated, "Nice pad. Looks like we'll have a fun weekend here." That was my attempt at being cool and understating the prospect of our first weekend together.

She let out some kind of Southern whoop, danced into the center of the living room, twirled a couple of times and yelped, "It's all ours for the weekend!"

With my back to the door, I did another one-eighty scan of the living room, still flat footed in the foyer, still in shock, but recovery was imminent, and I was suddenly thirsty. I smiled broadly and asked, "Got wine?"

"Yeah, let's open some now! Daddy loves wine, so I'm sure anything we open will be really good." Another whoop flew out of her: "Let the party begin!"

Julie was fun that way, and no doubt, the wine would be good.

She popped two bottles of a vintage French cabernet: one for spilling into our glasses for instant gratification and the other left open on the bar to breathe, while it stood on call following the inevitable draining of the first bottle. A bottle only held four glasses, after all, so there was no doubt we'd get to it at some point.

The sunset was in its final stages, very close to the point where people in Key West would be flooding into Mallory Square, on the wharf, and jockeying for a vantage point in a hubbub of hope to see the green flash that only occurred at the exact moment the sun's top edge dipped below the horizon. We said nothing as we stared intensely at the sun's impending disappearance, side by side with freshly poured glasses in hand, at the edge of the bar in front of a big picture window. The sun dipped out of sight, and its denouement showed us nothing other than the spellbinding beauty of that earthly moment when the day slips into dusk. Moments later, Julie disappeared down a long hallway, calling out to me that she had to make a phone call and to make myself comfortable. Easy enough! Glass and bottle in hand, and with the greatest of care not to spill a drop, I navigated the maze of white on white on white of the living room to get to the patio between the house and the pool.

The western horizon was becoming kaleidoscopic with the final vestiges of the sunken sun. The view from the patio into the Gulf was magnificent. The house was magnificent. And, yes, Julie was magnificent. We were going to have a lot of fun, and what a great place to get to know her better. I smiled to myself, convinced that I was, indeed, going to get to know her a lot better, in many ways. I inhaled the moist salty air that was blowing in with the surf and sipped my wine, as the bowl of my glass captured the golden glow coming off the horizon. I sunk into my very cushy patio chair, which was white, of course, feeling on top of the world, to wait for Julie's return.

I missed the green flash. I always do, and I'm not sure there really is such a thing. And now I was missing Julie. Maybe twenty minutes had passed since her disappearance. I was well into my second glass of cab, but willing to be patient. It must have been an important call, and I didn't see any need to interrupt. She would show up when she was done, and that was good enough for me.

I continued to wait without complaint while watching a sky full of blues, indigos, and purples wash over golden-orange wisps of clouds, disappearing in the fading light of errant rays. And then all of it faded with the passage of the hour, into the infinite depths of the darkening sky overhead. Slowly, the first evening star made an appearance, its light growing by the minute, high over the Gulf of Mexico. Then one star after another...and another...until the sky was full of them.

It had been two hours since Julie's departure down the hall. My patience, driven so long by an overbearing commitment to politeness, had run out. The bottle of wine that sat on the side table next to me was long gone. It was now completely dark outside, and without any lights on in the living room, darkness had the run of the house too. It was time to find her.

I entered the house through the door that I'd used earlier, and with my first step, I slid my hand along the wall just off the door frame, hopeful of connecting with a light switch panel. There was none there. I cautiously moved forward and to the right, taking small steps and opening my eyes as much as possible for a sighting of the silhouette of a lamp, any lamp. I couldn't believe how dark it was, and I had a funny flash of an idea that I was moving like a burglar, so out of place in this museum of a house. Within fifteen feet of the door, I located a table and the vague presence of a lamp on it, but groped for it cautiously, not knowing what else was on the table. Surely the only things on any of the tables in this house were really expensive lamps and really expensive fragile things. Fragile things from Venice. And Steuben. Maybe the Ming Dynasty.

With the quick twist of my thumb and forefinger on a switch, a lamp lit up the room, much to my relief. I suddenly no longer felt like a burglar and continued my mission to find Julie. I turned in the direction of the hallway, snapping wall switches along the way, lighting my path into a wing of the house. I was seeking an open door, and listening for a voice talking on the phone. I passed one closed door after another, all the way to the end, and none of them betrayed a voice in the rooms behind them.

"Julie?" I called out her name gently at first, then upped the volume a bit as I stood still listening for a reply. Still nothing, as I stood perplexed at the end of the hallway. I tried one more call out, almost a yell, "Julie!" Again, nothing. How strange! Now I was feeling weird and thinking I was going to slip back into that creepy burglar feeling. Here I was in a strange house, seemingly by myself, but I couldn't have been by myself, right?

I began opening doors leading into dark bedrooms and dens and sitting rooms, illuminating each one with the flip of a switch. "Why?" I asked myself, "if they are dark, did I think I would find Julie in one of them?" There were a lot of doors, and after about six or seven fruitless attempts, I stopped opening them and collected my thoughts. There must have been another seven or eight that I hadn't tried, but by then, it occurred to me that I should go to the front door to see if her car was still there. This made me feel really weird because I couldn't imagine it wouldn't be there. What did that mean? Did I think she just got in the car and drove away without saying anything to me? My imagination was becoming fertile, and the line of possible scenarios quickly got pretty long.

I picked up my pace as I approached the foyer, anxious to get some enlightenment. A quick flick of some wall switches in the foyer caused the front entrance to light up and, along with it, the carriage lamps flanking the outside of the front door. The car was there, parked exactly where we had left it, but there was no sign of Julie. I was moving beyond a weird feeling and actually started getting that silly Twilight Zone feeling. Here I am, alone in some mansion of mansions, invited into this never-seen-before space by a woman that I didn't really know, not really, really know. And she disappears and, in fact, hasn't been around for a couple of hours, ever since she walked off to make a phone call and fell down a rabbit hole.

Maybe something awful happened to her. Maybe she fainted, tripped and hit her head, had a heart attack, fell down some stairs, got amnesia and walked away, went into an epileptic coma, wandered off the property with dementia, is playing hide and seek, slipped into a catatonic state, ditched me, is waiting in a dark room for me with a butcher knife to drive into my heart. Oh yeah, my imagination was suddenly running wild! I mentally chastised myself for all these crazy thoughts and muttered, "Get a grip, Tom." My name softly echoed in the room.

I returned to the hallway where I had last seen her and tried the remaining untested doors, again flicking on a light in each one and ignoring the logical question, Why would I find her in a dark room?

With the flick of the light switch in the second to last room, I found her! She was immobile on a king bed, on her back, arms akimbo, and—what? dead? unconscious? asleep? Forever too polite, I approached her and whispered her name, "Julie?" I paused for a couple of heartbeats and upped the volume a bit, "Julie?" She was breathing, so dead was out.

She moaned, which was good because it meant she wasn't unconscious—another bad possibility eliminated. But, I asked myself, "Was she dying? Was she in jeopardy? Was she ill? Was she in a life-threatening condition?" All these thoughts raced through my head, spurred by the growing possibilities in my imagination and, of course, genuine concern. Over two hours had passed since she had walked off to make that call. What was the cause of this alarming state?

I sat on the bed alongside her. It shifted under my weight, and Julie moaned again, apparently aware, though barely, of my presence—or someone's. I leaned forward to whisper her name, when I felt the wash of her breath on my face and the overwhelming blowback of that sweet scent of a cabernet. That's when I noticed an empty glass on the bedside table, the one she had filled in the kitchen when we arrived nearly three hours ago. And alongside the empty glass was an empty bottle of cabernet—probably that second bottle she had opened in the kitchen. She was drunk and, apparently, had passed out. That was a lot of wine to consume by someone so petite—or large. Or anyone on a weekend date for the first time. What was she thinking!

"Now what?" is the question I silently asked myself, totally perplexed. This event certainly cleared the evening's agenda of everything, including conversation. The room wasn't cold, and there were no drafts that I could detect, so I didn't worry about covering her up. I certainly wasn't going to get her out of her clothes and tuck her in. I was sure she would be out for the night, or a good part of it anyway. I stood up, walked to the door, turned the lights out, and left, softly closing the door behind me and ending whatever thoughts I'd had for a fun evening. All this proved to me that whatever one envisions for an evening on a date is the one thing that definitely won't happen. So much for romance—and welcome to the Twilight Zone! It was all too weird.

I went out to her car, careful not to lock myself out of the house, and grabbed my suitcase, after having left it behind in the excitement of our arrival. The night was over for us, and even though I was on west coast time, the traveling had done me in or, more likely, the suspense and discovery of the last hour had exhausted me enough that I had to find a bed for myself. I was feeling the wine I'd had earlier. I ducked into one of the previously discovered bedrooms, brushed my teeth, stripped, and climbed into bed, wondering what the conversation would be like with Julie in the morning. I wondered about that for quite a bit, maybe for an hour, maybe two, until I fell asleep—in the museum.

I awoke with the light of a Florida morning coming through my window. It was gray with a yellow tint, enough yellow in it to carry the promise of a hot, steamy day ahead. I felt like crap on the heels of a lot of traveling and a short night of not very good sleep. The Julie Problem was running roughshod over me. It slapped me in the face before I had both eyes open, as if it had been hovering over me all night, just waiting for me to stir. I rolled out of bed, ambled into and out of the bathroom, after skipping a shower, and slid into my tired clothes. But they weren't as tired as I was. I went into the hallway toward Julie's room. Her door was closed. A gentle knock didn't do any good, so I poked my nose through a couple of inches of open door. She wasn't on the bed, but I could hear the shower running, so I backed out, silently closed the door, and decided to wait in the living room, not far from where she had left me twelve hours ago.

Thirty minutes later, Julie floated into the room on a silent current of air, and upon seeing me sitting motionless on a couch in the middle of the room, froze in her bare feet twenty feet in front of me, as if wanting to be invisible. If I hadn't been looking up, I wouldn't have noticed her. Now I was looking right into an angel's face, who didn't know what to do. She must have been surprised by suddenly discovering my presence, but her face didn't show it. I think she was expecting to find me in the kitchen or maybe the patio or maybe not in the house at all, but not motionless in the middle of the museum in a suspended state of angst, obviously waiting for her. For a very long five seconds, her face was expressionless, before it was overcome by a sheepish please-forgive-me grin. I'm sure that's what it was, but I was equally sure I wasn't feeling much like forgiving her. With the morning sun coming full bore through the eastern windows, my anger and disappointment rose with it. And then I rose to my feet but didn't approach her.

"This isn't going to work," I stated loud and clear. She stood across the room, taking it, without a response. I continued, "I'd like you to take me to the airport. I'll fly home today." Her forgive-me expression dropped off and was quickly replaced by a curl of her lower lip and the flooding of her eyes with tears. They began to run down her face. She didn't move. I went to her slowly and put

164

my arms around her, with her face moving into my sternum. All I could see was a pile of blonde hair well below my chin, sitting on some gently heaving shoulders.

"I don't know what last night was all about," I said softly, "but whatever it was, it can't be good." I waited a few seconds before continuing: "Look, we hardly know each other, but that bottle thing…" I groped for the right words, and then continued, "The fact that you passed out on the bed is not something I can deal with. I can't help you with that." I held on to her, but no response was forthcoming, just the muted sound of her whimpering, maybe in despair. Finally, Julie pushed back just enough to keep my arms around her and make enough room for her to look up. Her eyes were red and saturated with tears yet to fall. My heart pinged with her pain.

"I had to call my sister," she croaked. "She's having problems and she needed me."

This was a response I hadn't expected, mostly because it didn't do anything to explain Julie's behavior.

"And?" I asked, willing her to continue, while thinking that something more like an explanation for her behavior needed to follow. But other than a few snuffles, no further words followed. Her face disappeared again into my chest, and she whimpered some more. I could feel my shirt getting wet where her face was pressed into me.

I repeated my opening line, as if treading on thin ice in unknown territory, "This isn't going to work, Julie. I'm sorry." My arms fell to my side, but she continued to clutch me, her arms around my waist, clinging tightly. At this point, I was shifting out of a state of consolation to impending awkwardness. For the first time, I noticed the coffered ceiling of the museum. It was an intense latticework of three-foot square panels, each painted in ivory with accents of olive and sage greens. My mind started estimating the total number of panels. It looked as if there were about fifteen across the room and maybe thirty in length and...

"Julie?" I whispered, in a sing song voice that I thought would get her attention without being too intrusive. I gently pushed back on her shoulders, seeking a little separation so we could talk eye to eye. "Julie," I repeated, "let's sit down and talk about this." Thankfully, she was compliant. We would be more comfortable sitting down. I was sure of it and, besides, I was done counting. There were four hundred and seventy-two coffers in the museum's ceiling.

Julie and I talked on the couch for an hour. I bought into her tearful regret—what she called "slippage," as a consequence of a difficult relationship with her sister, which was beyond my understanding. At any rate, Julie assured me that her episode with excessive consumption the previous night was a one-time folly on her part. Whatever it was, it certainly was a red flag if we were to continue dating. Some little voice in me was saying something about that.

I don't know how it happened, but inside of two hours I got over it, and we committed to having a fun weekend together, as we had planned, despite the horrible start.

All of the qualities that had drawn me to her prevailed, and that was the beginning of our relationship, which lasted fifteen months. Distance finally did us in, although our breakup wasn't really as simple as that. Distance is the reason I give for its demise, which doesn't really mean much because, as everyone knows, there's his story and there's her story—and then there's the truth, somewhere in between.

CHAPTER 11: A Party in Napa Valley

Her name was Jill.

It was Friday noon, and I was driving eighty miles an hour—five over—to the Sacramento airport to pick her up for a weekend as my houseguest in Napa Valley. In less than an hour, I would be meeting her for the first time, without even having seen a picture of her! It happened so fast—only four hours earlier—in a phone conversation with my friend Peter, who lives in Los Angeles. The conversation was still fresh in my mind. It's amazing how quickly things can happen in one's life, especially in the dating world.

When Peter called me that morning, he and I played catch up ball, swapping updates on our lives and loved ones before he got to the real purpose of his call: to fix me up with a friend of his in L.A., and waste no time doing it. Wasting no time meant that Peter and his friend Jill thought it'd be great if she flew up that morning for a fun weekend with me. Peter told me that he had already sold her on the idea of me. Then he sold me on the idea of her. I didn't need much in the way of convincing. I didn't have a date that weekend, but I did have an

168

invitation to a very cool party that night, which I thought might be more fun with a date.

Five minutes after talking to Peter, I was talking to Jill for the first time. She had a terrific voice, which was perky, fun, and sexy, all at the same time. She said I didn't sound like a pervert, a weirdo, a bore, or overbearing. I guess women and men listen for different things in a voice, although she eventually said I had a nice voice and sounded like a nice person. How nice for me. We laughed enough in those first minutes and, consequently, knew we'd get along. It was a go. We hit it off as much as two people could in ten minutes on the phone talking to each other for the first time.

Five minutes after talking to Jill, I was booking a flight for her on Southwest. I called her back and gave her the details of the reservation that I'd made in her name and hung up. I think Peter's endorsement had laid sufficient groundwork for what we needed to know. Jill had less than three hours to pack and get to the airport for a timely flight out of LAX to Sacramento to meet me. It was really spontaneous and seemed like a good idea. Jill sounded like a lot of fun, and she was excited about meeting me.

We both might have just signed off on a weekend of mutually assured destruction, I mused. You never know what'll happen on a blind date—all kinds of possibilities float around in the universe, something I learned over the years from a lot of blind dates. A lot. We both knew there were risks, but—hey—everything pointed to a good time, so we both jumped feet first into the fire, hopeful that we'd have a fantastic weekend together and, possibly, that it would be the first in a string of pearls. I wouldn't be wrong in saying we were both hopeful. Spontaneous behavior can lead to spontaneous combustion, which could be good if it means the relationship gets really hot; but it could be bad, too, if it means the relationship blows up like an improvised explosive device.

I moved into the arrivals lane and approached the sidewalk outside the Southwest baggage area at the Sacramento airport. I saw a woman who fit Peter's description exactly. She was about five four and pretty, with long blonde hair. She had a petite frame, which Peter described as "delightfully top heavy." She was somewhere in her mid-thirties, like Peter, and about ten years younger than me. It was Jill. She saw the flash of my brights on my black Suburban as I coasted up to her and her very large suitcase, which was a double-wide on wheels and, no doubt, packed with a closet full of clothes. Peter said Jill might be a bit on the side of high maintenance, but he wasn't sure. He didn't have enough data points on that.

I let it go as the only possible red flag that came up. It was easy to ignore because she sounded perfect for a fun weekend and, as one of Peter's single female friends in L.A., she had enough good qualities that might even make for a good girlfriend. She was a known quantity, at least to Peter. Like I said, I was hopeful, and how could we not have a fun weekend in Napa Valley!

I got out and walked around the front of my car, stepped onto the curb, and warmly greeted Jill, totally content with my first impression of her. Hugging felt too forward, and our height difference made it a tad too awkward for this first meeting. Instead, I threw out an upbeat, "Hi, you must be Jill!" and followed it with a quick handshake and a double handed grab at the suitcase. All of this enhanced the feeling that we were on some kind of adventure, already having fun and with no time to waste. She certainly worked for me visually, and she probably had the same assessment of me. It's not as if either of us would say, "Hey, this isn't going to work for me. Let's just say goodbye now." Of all the possibilities in the universe, I was pretty sure that wasn't one of them.

I quickly stuffed her double-wide into the backseat before opening the door for her, which she waited for me to do. That waiting thing was good. It showed that she appreciated a gentleman, or at least expected one. I liked that because I am a gentleman. With a supportive hand engulfing one of hers, I helped her climb the steep grade into the front seat and gently closed the door. Gentle is a nice touch. Sometimes I even surprise myself with how sensitive I can be.

The ninety-minute drive back to my place in the heart of Napa Valley was delightful. We talked nonstop about everything we each wanted the other person to know and asked everything we thought we had to know, at least for starters. Surprisingly, Jill had never been to Napa, so when we entered the valley after an hour in the car, I told her about its evolution from the early hippie days in winemaking through the years it transformed itself into a slice of Italy with the addition of miles of fieldstone walls, accents of Italian cypress trees, rows and rows of olive trees, and of course the ubiquitous Tuscan influences in residential architecture.

The wineries themselves had a different kind of architectural influence. Their design was driven by the need to be memorable, unique, and spectacularly inviting, which was understandable, given the importance of onsite sales to their bottom line. As every valley resident knew, and contrary to visitors' expectations, the wine sold in the wineries wasn't a bargain; Safeway prices were always better. The only reason to buy wine at a Napa winery was because it wasn't available anywhere else, although souvenirs were appropriate as an acceptable reason to buy, but not by the case.

I turned down Ragatz Lane, two miles south of Yountville. It was a dead-end lane of ten aging and dated ranch houses that were being overlooked in the renovation craze, which was feverishly underway. My home, which was at the very end of the lane, was the exception. I had done a major renovation on it three years earlier. It was set deep into the lot by a long driveway, cut off from the street's flotsam by a thick border of giant redwoods and bounded by a backyard of vineyards and a creek running on one side, creating an impression that it was apart from everything else in the neighborhood and in its own little world. After a drive down the lane, its facade was a very pleasant surprise to everyone, and Jill was very pleasantly surprised when I pulled into the driveway. It was all quite impressive. Yep, you guessed it: I redesigned the house to look like a mini-Tuscan manor, complete with Italian Cypress trees framing the corners of the house and olive trees lining the driveway. I was living the Napa Valley dream, except I didn't own a winery.

When we entered the house, Jill *oohed* and *ahhed* over the decor, trailing me as I hauled her two-wheeled closet into the guest suite, where I pointed out the amenities and left her for a few minutes to unpack. While I waited for her return to the great room, I poured a couple of glasses of one of my favorite Sauvignon Blanc labels to accompany a platter of camembert and brie, a small dish of Kalamata olives, a delicious black olive tapenade from Spain, some sweet red peppercini peppers, and of course some water crackers.

I elected to entertain Jill on my back patio in the mid-afternoon until it was time to go to a very fancy dinner party that a friend of mine was having up valley that night to celebrate his fortieth birthday. By the time Jill returned, I had a display set out for us on the dining table on the back patio, which was like what you'd see in a gourmet magazine, with only the lap pool between us and the vineyards. It was one of the many perfect settings in Napa Valley, this one happening on a perfectly sunny September day. It was all so perfect. Thankfully, the redwoods on the western border of my lot shaded us from the direct rays of the waning summer's sun and transported us into a sun-dappled state of nirvana as we got to know each other even better.

I told her that I'd grown up in Wisconsin, which made me a Midwest boy with Midwest values, and that I'd gone to college at Indiana University and stayed there for an MBA before taking my first job in an advertising agency in New York City. She was surprised to learn that after New York, I had lived in Atlanta, Dallas, and San Francisco before moving to Napa. It seemed like a lot of places to her. I didn't mention a summer in Paris. Jill grew up in Orange County. As a kid growing up in Wisconsin, I told her that I'd never imagined that I'd have a date with a California girl. The Beach Boys made California girls seem like they were from another world— because they were. And I told her that I certainly would never have guessed that someday I'd be living in California.

She said that she'd gone to the California State University in Northridge in L.A., and ever since, she's lived in Santa Monica. I noticed that she didn't say she "graduated" from Northridge, only that she went there, so I assumed she didn't have a college degree. That was a shame, I thought to myself, but not a big deal, not really, so I didn't press. I safely concluded that she was a California girl through and through—whatever that meant—because she had never lived anywhere else. I suppose I should have asked her if she surfed; that was part of my California girl image. Thank you, Beach Boys.

Two hours passed in two minutes. Suddenly, it was time to prep for the next event. I wanted to allow Jill plenty of time to get ready for the dinner party. I gave her an hour and a half until departure for our twenty-five minute drive up the valley. From our first conversation, she already knew she'd need something dressy for tonight's party. I suggested attire that was casually elegant for a dinner alfresco, with a light sweater or jacket for temperatures that would be dropping as the evening wore on. I retired to my bedroom at the top of the spiral staircase, which was off the living room side of the great room, over the guest quarters. That left me with more than enough time to get ready, so I turned on the TV to drown out my call to Peter. He wasn't in, but I left a voice message expressing my deep gratitude for this wonderful and promising fix-up, named Jill, and then watched the news before I got dressed.

Two hours later, Jill still wasn't ready. When I called down the hall for her status, she called out, "In a minute!"

It was a dinner party, and I hated to be late for dinner parties, but I was still thinking we'd make it in time for the seating. I fixed myself a roadie for the drive up, since I was pretty sure we'd be missing the cocktail hour preceding dinner. Yes, that's right—a cocktail. People living in Napa Valley didn't always drink wine. The summer wasn't over, and my choice in cocktails was a gin and diet tonic with a lime, so that's what I was fixing when Jill made her entrance.

One look at her, and I thought instantly that it was worth the wait. She had on a silky summer dress. It was above the knee and well below the collar bone, which is to say, it was cut very low and, on Jill, very low was what I called sea level, meaning you could see a lot. Not meaning to dwell on this particular design element, but I have to say that Jill had a lot to see, so consider me lucky. The only thing that saved her from house arrest was the black cashmere cardigan she was wearing. Besides covering her shoulders, it covered a lot. She'd be in trouble if the temperature dropped more than five degrees, something all men at the party would be hoping for when they saw her.

"Wow, Jill," I exclaimed, "You look fantastic!" It was no exaggeration, and I could I tell she knew it and clearly understood what I meant when I said it was a fancy party. She'd do just fine even if she had lockjaw all evening. Some dates, you know, are better with lockjaw. Jill wasn't one of them.

I told her about my friends Bill and Susan, who were hosting the party. It was Bill's fortieth and, as it turned out, a celebration for his meteoric success as well. Their house was in the hills above St. Helena, a town in Napa Valley that is in total denial that it's something other than a collection of high-priced tourist boutiques. It was their second home; their first was in Pacific Heights. By anyone's measure, Bill and Susan's second home was everybody else's idea of a dream home. It was even Bill and Susan's idea of a dream home. Inspired by a French

Provincial home that Bill loved in Shaker Heights, Ohio, the town he grew up in, it had to be at least eight thousand square feet of tasteful country luxe décor, perched on a hill with a southern view that ran fifty miles over the valley to San Francisco Bay. It was idyllic in a subtly opulent way, and Bill and Susan were the perfect hosts and hugely likable for all kinds of reasons. They would like Jill; I was pretty sure of that. I liked Jill; I was also pretty sure of that.

We surrendered our car to the valet service moments before everyone was being seated. Jill and I were next to each other at a table mixed with some people I knew and some I didn't. As it turned out, it was a selection of people that were all great fun and made for stimulating conversations in every direction. Jill held her own and, like me, was loving every minute. Halfway into dinner, the birthday toasts began and merriment was rampant. Bill delivered a wonderful and short review of his very interesting adult life. A chorus of the birthday song followed, and then the live band kicked in for dancing into the night, which took place on a platform under strings of paper lantern lights by the pool house.

It's a shame not to get into details of this exquisitely fun party, but suffice it to say, Jill was a terrific date throughout the evening. She mingled with and without me, returning to my side before I ever started missing her and easily convinced me that I was the best date she had had in a long time. We were mutually in sync on that thought. The hours flew by, and the clock struck midnight, which is pretty late for Napa. By then, we had all been pushed indoors by the chilly air, not wanting to call it a night.

When Jill and I got back to my house, we nixed a night cap, but agreed that a soak in the hot tub was the perfect way to end the evening. I bought into that, though other perfect endings came to mind. I liked Jill, and we had plenty of time left in the weekend to fool around. I decided that the best course of action on this first night together was no action, so to speak. She hadn't brought a bathing suit for the hot tub, and going native apparently wasn't in the cards, so she climbed in wearing a black t-shirt I offered gallantly.

We weren't in the hot tub for long, but long enough to laugh some more and share some secrets. The latter was an automatic, as I always felt that "truth tub" was just as descriptive as hot tub. In what we knew would be the final minute or two in the tub, we each expressed the truth about our feelings for each other in no other way than simply a first kiss. And, like every first kiss shared by two people intensely interested in each other, there was an unbearable joy from the indescribable sensation that occurs in that infinitesimally small space between the anticipation of a kiss and the actual kiss.

For us, time stopped for a very long kiss. It was a blissful moment shared. It sealed a perfect evening together and carried the promise of more of that tomorrow. We climbed out of the tub, toweled off, went inside while still a little wet, grabbed some bottled water out of the Sub-Zero, said goodnight, and went to our separate bedrooms. Tired but happy, we both looked forward to another day together. And, surely, another night.

I slept late into the morning, that is, late for me, which was about nine. I usually get up with the sun, but that's because I'm usually in bed before two in the morning, which was about the time I'd hit the light in my bedroom the previous night. I brushed my teeth, then quietly made my way down the spiral staircase. It's made of metal, so it has a tendency to put out a faint echo, which is not so faint if I clump down in a run with hard-soled shoes. I was barefoot, guided by my desire for a large glass of cold orange juice followed by a sixteen-ounce bottle of Diet Coke. I don't drink coffee, so I depend on the Coke to launch me into a higher level of awareness. It sounds very Zen. The O.J. was downed in a minute, and I took the bottle of high octane fuel back upstairs with me so that I could work on it through the news on TV. I left my bedroom door open, on alert for Jill's footsteps padding into the great room.

After an hour of silence downstairs, I slipped into my running gear, wrote a note for Jill, and left the house for a jog along a perfectly suitable path, which tractors had carved through the vineyards. The sun was already hot. Even without it, I would have been soaked in sweat from my hour-long run. I stealthily entered the house, in deference to the possibility that Jill might still be sleeping, but half expecting to see her fixing herself some coffee, which I'd left on the counter before my run. The coffee was untouched, and she was not in sight. "A sleeper," I thought to myself, and why not—we had a big night, she's on vacation, and floating on a new mattress with six hundred thread count cotton sheets and a light down comforter. It sounded so good that I thought for a moment I should climb into bed with her. I dismissed the thought, but playfully entertained the idea that I might climb into her bed tomorrow morning, if she's not already in mine.

I took a shower, dressed for success, and returned to the kitchen to nibble out of a package of Entemann's Danish, an emergency breakfast that I pulled from the pantry, having skipped the cheese omelet, bacon, and English muffins I would have prepared for the two of us in the morning, had there been two of us in the morning. I went out to the patio to read *The New York Times* and breathe in the crystal clear and fragrant air of the Valley, filtered by the morning mists and delivered fresh daily from the Pacific Ocean. At a few minutes past noon, I wandered back into the house for another hit of Entemann's, wondering if I'd ever see Jill again. With a mouthful of Danish decadence, I heard some water rush through some hidden pipe, telling me that the guest room shower just went on. Life with Jill prevails!

Forty minutes later, while I was still working through the paper, and half of the contents of the Entemann's box was missing, Jill emerged onto the patio with a coffee cup in one hand and some Danish on a paper towel in the other. She was dressed in hot pink capri pants, topped with a white sleeveless cotton blouse, coordinated with shoes that had only a thin pink strap, which made her look barefoot but four inches taller. Her makeup and hair looked like she was ready for a TV commercial for Silky Something, and she could have walked on stage for the talent portion of a beauty pageant, though I didn't know her well enough yet to know what her talent was.

I motioned for her to sit on the lounge chair next to me, both of us then looking contentedly over the lap pool and out over the vines to the eastern ridge of the mountains that formed one boundary of the valley. The sun was overhead and not too hot yet, although it would be in a couple of hours. So, we enjoyed the magnificent setting and continued with the same kind of animation in our conversations that we had going for us the day before. Jill was easy to talk to. She had a lot to say, which made it easy for me to be a good listener, and she freely spoke her mind. All these were qualities I liked, so I stretched out on the lounge chair, fully at ease with her, and licked the frosting off my fingers from my last bit of Entemann's.

As we talked on the patio, we ran through topics like a surfer runs through channels, taking in tidbits of information about each other from whatever came to mind. I got around to asking her about her dating life, which I've found to be an easy and interesting topic for anyone and often leads to all kinds of stories.

"Tell me, Jill, about the kind of man you want to be with, you know, the kind you see yourself in love with. What's he like?"

"Oh, that's easy," she replied without hesitation. "I've been visualizing him for a long time. You want me to start with his looks?"

"Sure," is all I could say, and it's all I needed to say, as her tone indicated she was clearly eager to talk about this guy. This should be interesting because I was wondering if she knew who she was talking to and if there would be much of a resemblance between her Mr. Right and the guy *on* her right.

"He's tall, at least six feet tall," was her opening line, and that was good to know because I'm six three. She continued without missing a beat: "I like tall men. Even though I'm short, I want to be with a tall man. I don't know why exactly. I just like tall men."

I interrupted, thinking I was being witty and provocative, but being neither, "Does that work for dancing?"

"What do you mean?"

"Well, the height difference. Are you okay with putting your chin on his sternum?"

"On his what?"

"His sternum," I repeated and said, "This," as I thumped the center of my chest a couple of times."

"Oh, like for slow dancing?"

"Yeah, for slow dancing," I said.

"I don't like slow dancing," she said.

I didn't say anything. She moved on.

"And, of course, he's got to have a good build—you know, in really good shape. But he doesn't have to have, like, muscleman muscles; that's a turn off." She obviously paused to visualize this guy. "Good abs would be good. Oh, and he should have good hands, too. I pay a lot of attention to hands."

I interrupted again, placing a hand over my forehead and leaning forward, as if in a gesture of deep thought, so that she couldn't miss my hand on my head, and asked, "Really, he's gotta have good hands? That's important, huh?" With that, I playfully waved my other hand in front of her face. She looked at me funny and didn't get what I was doing. Since my antics had elicited no comment, I guessed she didn't really pay a lot of attention to hands. That's a shame, as I've been told I have good hands. I let it go and reclined again on the couch, like a psychiatrist's patient, but I decided to let the shrink do all the talking.

Her next statement really got my attention. She was looking far away, caught up in this visualization exercise when she said, "I'd like him to have a head of thick, dark hair so that I can play with it." She sighed over that vision and continued, "I want to run my fingers through it." Upon hearing that, I'm totally sure she's forgotten who's sitting next to her because I'm bald. I let it go, telling myself that no one's perfect, not that not having hair isn't perfect. I guess this just meant that I wasn't perfect for her. She continued her description of Mr. Right, speaking out of a stream of consciousness:

"Of course he'd have to like a lot of the things I like. Having stuff in common is really important, but I don't mind if we have some differences. Differences are good, in some things. I don't care about politics or religion, but we should think a lot alike, you know, believe in the same things and like to go to Italy. I love Italy. I love Rome. I love everything over there. Yeah, we could travel a lot and stay at all the best hotels."

I'm thinking we were still in sync, in a simple way, aside from the hair thing. Nothing she said so far was silly, a deal-breaker, or unreasonable, although the part about staying in the best hotels made me think about the hotels I usually stayed in when I traveled. I winced a bit. They were nice, but they definitely were not the best hotels. Even so, I shared the dream: Maybe we would stay in the best hotels someday. Maybe I could afford them someday. The stream of consciousness was flowing out of her now like Niagara Falls going over the edge.

"I love great hotels—not just in Italy. I love 'em everywhere. Oh, and I love room service. Sometimes I just want to spend the whole day in bed and get treated like a princess."

The princess statement made my ears perk up, like radar picking up a UFO. Now that was a statement that planted the first seed of serious doubt that Jill and I were destined to be together.

"Well, not all day, of course," she flowed, "I want to spend the afternoons shopping. I love shopping—anywhere and everywhere. I love to shop. I love nice clothes. And nice things. I don't care what they cost. I can't help it."

The flow of her words continued, and I suddenly envisioned her caught up in it, in a barrel, going over Niagara Falls.

"I mean, I care about money, of course, but the man for me would have so much that he would just want me to be happy, to have anything I want. I could spend entire afternoons on Rodeo Drive and not worry about a thing."

That seed of serious doubt was now rapidly germinating. It looked to me like a study in time-lapsed photography.

"Oh, he would be so wonderful to me," she said, in a tone that made me think she was going even deeper into her fantasy. "He would surprise me with beautiful jewelry, for no reason at all, just because he loved me so much."

The seed of doubt had grown into a sapling, and the time-lapsed photography was still in play.

I had to interrupt at this point, having been so quiet. I was rapidly moving into a state of shock. "Jill," I said, bursting out of my invisibility, "he sounds fantastic. Besides being a terrific guy and doing so many nice things for you, this guy must be hugely rich." I stated that with the intonation of a question, determined to get absolute clarification of her desires.

185

She didn't look at me. She was sitting with a straight back, almost in the Lotus position on the lounge chair, clearly energized by her vision, her eyes transfixed on the horizon. "Yeah, of course," she answered. "We'd live in Brentwood and be in all the photos at all the big society parties. I love those parties. I absolutely love them, with all the important people and celebrities. And they'd all want to talk to us and be seen with us. And...and maybe we'd have a second home in Hawaii, where we could entertain all our friends from around the world."

I had just witnessed a seed of doubt grow to the size of one of the redwoods in my back yard.

I was speechless over her idea of Mr. Right. He and I had very little in common. I didn't even think I'd like that guy. Besides, I was feeling so trumped by him that I easily concluded that Jill had just moved so far out of my realm that I'd rather press my hand on a hot plate than put a move on her. In ten short minutes, she'd gone from very attractive to a delusional space-head, totally mindless of where she was and who she was with. I may have been speechless, but I knew what to say—but I had to stand up to say it.

I rose and stepped in front of her, blocking her view of the vineyards and breaking off her fantasy. "Jill," I said in the tone of a pronouncement of great importance, "that is some kind of man you see for yourself." She nodded slightly, apparently in agreement, but also with a look of anticipation about what was next. Maybe she got an inkling that it wouldn't be good. I continued, "Listen," I paused for effect and then rolled into my verbal haymaker, "you're a very attractive woman, and we've had a lot of fun together in the short time we've known each other, but I'm not that man." Her eyes got big, and with that, I delivered the *coup de grace,* making an even bigger declarative statement: "I'm not the man for you, and I think you should fly back to Los Angeles on the first plane you can get."

Now it was her turn to be speechless. I looked into her eyes and saw them tearing up, and then made a move toward the house, calling out, "I'll call the airlines right now and get you on the next available flight." I paused at the patio door, having placed one foot already in the house, and said, "You can get back home in time to go out in L.A., and I suggest you pack now." I stepped into the house and went to my den to execute the plan, as if I'd just executed Jill. And, in a way, I had.

I noticed that she sat motionless on the lounge chair for several minutes. I think she was crying. At least it wasn't a shoulder-heaving cry, which would have been very difficult for me to take. Some might say I was a little harsh, but it was honest. We were clearly wasting each other's time. How could I possibly spend another evening with her after that monologue? I felt it was better for both of us to move forward. She could look for Mr. Right in Los Angeles that night, and I would be free of a relationship that clearly wasn't going anywhere.

I got her a ticket on the first possible plane back, which was leaving in three hours. She packed quickly, and I knew we could make it to the airport in time. It was only a ninety-minute drive, but it was the longest ninety-minute drive of my life, even at ten over. The silence was only broken by her snuffling, all the way to the airport. At the departures curb, I jumped out, opened her door, set her double-wide on the sidewalk next to her, and then stood before her, face to face. It was a good time to say as little as possible. I put my hands on her shoulders, looked her in her teary eyes, and said, "I'm sorry it turned out this way, Jill. I hope you meet Mr. Right one of these days. Like I said, I'm not that guy."

I got in the car and drove back to Napa Valley, unexpectedly dateless on a Saturday night. All I could think about was Jill and how right it had felt at the start—and how it suddenly felt so wrong. Of course she felt bad in the end, although I tell myself her tears were caused more by the shock of rejection than the actual rejection. I felt bad too, but I believed the break was best for both of us, however painful.

During the drive back, I called Peter and told him what had happened. "Bummer," he said. "She's a doll, but yeah, she's high maintenance. I just didn't know how high. Sorry," he said sympathetically, "real sorry it turned out that way. I guess you did the right thing. Anyway, I know Jill—she'll get over it. Probably by the time she lands."

We talked a little longer then signed off.

By the time I got back to Napa, I was over her.

ABOUT THE AUTHOR

Thomas Dunker was born in Milwaukee, Wisconsin and has lived in New York, Atlanta, Dallas, San Francisco, Napa, Scottsdale, and now lives in Sedona, Arizona. Besides being a writer, he is also an actor, an artist, and a marketing research consultant specializing in focus group moderation for Thomas Dunker & Associates, Inc. He is the author of *Confessions of a Dating Fool* and *A Love Story with a Little Heartbreak*. An excerpt from *Confessions of a Dating Fool* appears in this book. These books are available on Amazon.com. He paints under the name Tomaso DiTomaso. To view his work, please visit: www.TomasoPaintings.com.

OTHER BOOKS BY THOMAS DUNKER

The following books by Thomas Dunker are available on Amazon.com:

Confessions of a Dating Fool

Confessions of a Dating Fool is twelve short stories of dates written by a man confessing to his own must-be-shared dating experiences. In these amazing stories, based on actual experiences, the author bares his soul, shares his thoughts, and takes the reader with him on every meaningful step of each date in settings all around the world. Several readers have described it as *Sex and the City* from a man's point of view. Many have also called it a light, entertaining read that's totally captivating, making it a real page turner.

A common denominator of many of these stories is a surprising outcome. The element of surprise in the dating world is something everyone who has ever dated can relate to. The immense diversity in the human genome assures us that every date is an adventure into the limitless world of human emotions. These stories are funny, moving, adventurous, and even tragic. Some include sex, of course, as this is a book of confessions. Some also include the promise of sex and even the avoidance of it, much akin to everyone's dating experiences. This book takes the reader on a rollercoaster ride right through the last paragraph.

Dating stories, especially good ones of bad dates, are irresistible and often told again and again.

Confessions of a Dating Fool is a very light and quick read that has generated many a good laugh, a tear or two, and some terrific reader reviews on Amazon.com.

A Love Story with a Little Heartbreak

A Love Story with a Little Heartbreak is based on a true story of one woman's dream finally coming true not only against all odds but with the belief that the dream was suddenly lost forever only moments after its reality was at her fingertips. It is my mother's story. The story takes place in Chilton, a hamlet in the middle of the farming community of Central Wisconsin in 1945-1951. It is about the heartbreaking and instantaneous destruction of one woman's dream life – a life as part of a wonderfully romantic "it" couple - and, only with the strength and courage to survive enormous tragedy, does she recover the dream, a dream that she thought couldn't possibly happen again in her life and it happens with an unexpected ending that surpasses anyone's most hopeful expectations.

There are huge numbers of readers who love a good love story and there are huge numbers of readers who love to read about individuals who overcome all odds to achieve their personal dream. This story is a combination of the two. It not only leaves the reader with a happy ending (another reason this book is compelling), it is an ending that no one could guess, one that simply adds a little extra frosting to the cake.

AUTHOR'S NOTE

You might like to know that I will be happy to hear from you. It is best to simply email me. I can be quite good about returning emails. However, do not include attachments. I never open them. My email is ThomasJDunker@aol.com.

If you like my book, tell a friend. Better yet, buy a copy for a friend. People should know that authors love it when their books are purchased; it's so preferable to being asked for a copy. I will, of course, be happy to sign a copy for you. All you have to do is buy a copy, mail it to me with a check in the amount of $10 for shipping and handling and I'll see that you get the copy back with my signature and maybe a nice note along with it. My mailing address is P.O. Box 2189, Sedona, AZ 86339. Expect to wait 3-4 weeks for a signed copy to get back to you. Make your check payable to Thomas Dunker.